W9-CXU-183

GO FACTS **SCIENCE**

People and the Sea

Newbridge

People and the Sea

contents

People and the Sea
ISBN: 1-4007-3191-7

Published by
Newbridge Educational Publishing,
a Haights Cross Communications Company
11 East 26th Street, New York, NY 10010
www.newbridgeonline.com

Reviewer and Consultant: Marcia S. Freeman, Writing Specialist, Sarasota, FL

Written by Sharon Dalgleish, Garda Turner
Science Consultant: Dr. Will Edwards, School of Tropical Biology, James Cook University
Design and layout by The Modern Art Production Group
Photos by John Foxx, Photodisc, Stockbyte, Digital Stock, and Corel

Copyright © 2002 Blake Education, Australia

Enjoying the Sea

Swimming, boating, and fishing are some of the ways people have fun at the sea.

Some people make a splash, swimming in the sea or surfing on the waves. Others explore underwater worlds by snorkeling or even **scuba** diving.

People go boating in harbors and bays. They set sail in small boats, large cruisers, or sailing yachts. Some people like to leave the land far behind them.

Fresh sea air can make people hungry. Some pack a picnic and head for a seaside picnic ground. Others fish from boats, bridges, or the shore, and catch their own lunch!

The beach is a popular place for vacations.

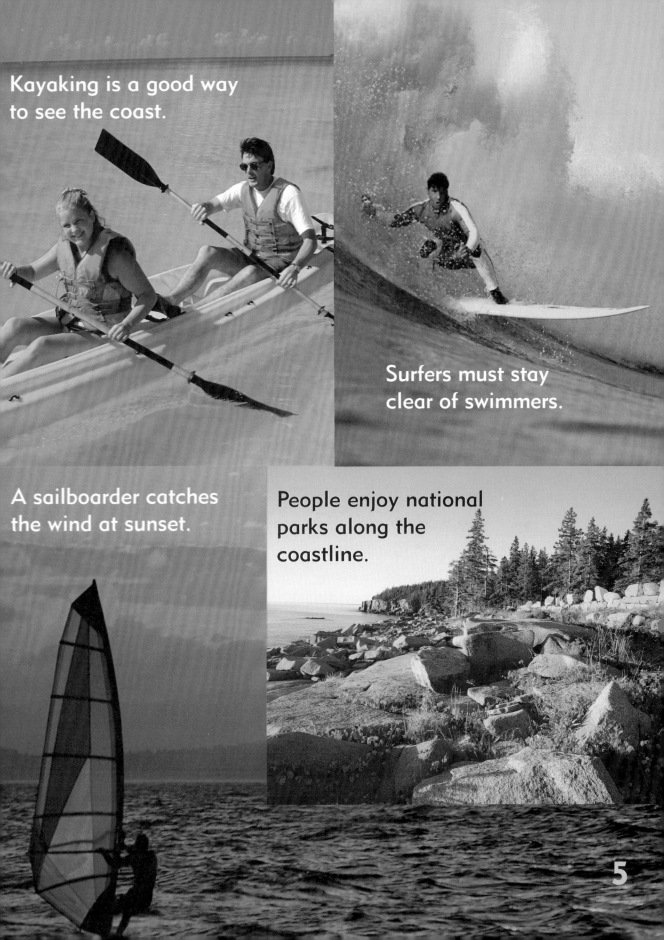

Kayaking is a good way to see the coast.

Surfers must stay clear of swimmers.

A sailboarder catches the wind at sunset.

People enjoy national parks along the coastline.

5

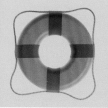

Safety at Sea

People enjoy different activities in and on the water. Simple rules help keep everyone safe.

At the beach, swimmers must follow the lifeguard's instructions. Surfboard riders must stay away from swimming areas. You should not swim if the waves are too rough or too big.

Scuba divers must check their equipment before going on each dive. They also learn hand signals so they can communicate under water. No one should dive alone.

Here are rules for people who like boating.

1. Make sure the boat is in good condition.

2. Plan your trip. Know where you are going and how long you will be. Tell someone of your plans.

3. Check the weather forecast. Make sure it is safe boating weather.

4. Wear a life jacket.

5. Carry a first aid kit, flashlight, distress flares, and a towrope. A radio or cell phone that lets you talk to someone on shore is a good idea.

Sunglasses protect your eyes and sunscreen protects your skin from sunburn.

People in boats have to watch for swimmers and people snorkeling.

People should never scuba dive alone.

Water Pressure

The water pressure in the deep sea is extremely high. Deep-sea water pressure would crush a person.

Try this experiment to see how **water pressure** increases as water gets deeper.

You will need:

- deep bucket
- straw or plastic tube
- water and food coloring
- balloon
- elastic band
- plastic bag

What to do:

1. Fill the bucket with water.

2. Attach the straw or plastic tube to the balloon with an elastic band. Fill the balloon with colored water.

3. Slowly lower the balloon into the bucket.

4. Watch the level of the colored water as you push the balloon deeper.

Now try this:

Wrap your hand in a plastic bag and place your hand under the water. You will feel the pressure increase as you push your hand deeper into the water.

Just below the surface the water pressure is low.

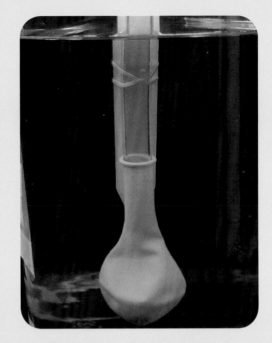

In deeper water, the pressure pushes the dye from the balloon into the tube.

The water pressure presses the plastic around your hand.

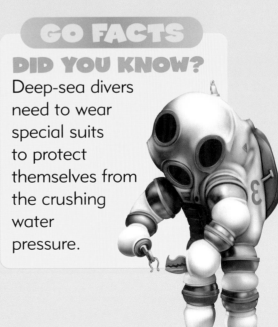

The Wild Sea

Some of the wildest storms on Earth begin at sea. When these storms hit land they can cause terrible destruction.

Hurricanes are huge, spinning storms. Their winds blow at 74 miles per hour or more and bring heavy rain. Most hurricanes form over warm seas during certain seasons. Many of these storms stay at sea, where they can be a danger to ships. When a hurricane hits land, it can cause terrible damage.

Weather scientists give hurricanes names that start with the letters of the alphabet in order from "A" onward. So if you hear of hurricane "Edward", you know it is the fifth serious tropical storm of the season. When a hurricane causes enough damage to make the news, its name is retired and never used again.

Tsunamis are giant waves that can be caused by earthquakes in the seabed. A volcano or landslide can also set off a tsunami. When a tsunami reaches shallow water close to land, the sea is sucked back from the shore and the waves come rushing back as a giant wall of water.

Spinning hurricanes can be seen from space.

Houses can be completely destroyed by hurricanes.

GO FACTS

DID YOU KNOW?

A tsunami can travel across deep oceans as fast as a jet plane! The waves can be up to 65 meters high when they hit land.

Working at Sea

If you're looking for smooth sailing, you may not want to work at sea. But the ocean is a great place to find a career full of excitement and discoveries.

An oil platform is like a small city at sea. Hundreds of people live on the platform surrounded by the drilling equipment, pumps, and power plant. The platform also has living areas with places to sleep, eat, and play.

A research ship is like a floating laboratory. A large research ship needs a crew of up to twenty people. Thirty different scientists may also live and work on-board.

Scientists study what lives in the water and on the sea floor. They also study how water moves in the oceans and how the oceans affect the **atmosphere**.

Scientist

Boats must be cleaned and repaired.

Divers explore ocean life.

Chefs can work at sea on cruise ships.

13

Explorers

From early times, people have set sail on the oceans to explore the unknown. Some explorers looked for new lands to settle. Others looked for fame, treasure, or adventure.

More than 3,000 years ago people explored the Pacific Ocean. Traveling in small canoes, people used the stars to help them find their way. By the early 1200s the magnetic compass had been invented. Sailors could then **navigate** more easily. Even so, the journeys were still filled with danger.

The 1400s were an age of discovery. Explorers such as Marco Polo and Christopher Columbus discovered new trade routes and lands they had never seen before. Traders bought and sold cloth, food, metals, and especially spices like pepper and cinnamon. Storms, pirates, and hidden reefs caused some ships to sink. Today, adventurers go in search of the sunken treasure!

Stormy seas and rocky coasts made sailing to new lands dangerous.

Early boats were very simple.

Galleons were used as warships and for trade from the 1400s to the 1600s.

GO FACTS

DID YOU KNOW?

Ferdinand Magellan's ships were the first to sail around the world. Magellan set sail from Spain in 1519 with five ships. In 1522, one of his ships made it home.

Ocean Highways

World trade depends on ships to carry goods. Ocean and sea routes are like water highways. Ships follow special shipping lanes around the world.

Each day tankers carry oil from the North Sea and the Middle East to the rest of the world. Bulk carriers transport iron ore, coal, food, and manufactured goods from one country to another. Cruise ships carry passengers on vacation.

With all this traffic, the ocean highways can get very busy. There is a danger of ships running into each other. To solve the problem, ships have **radar** and **sonar** equipment. They also use radio waves sent via **satellite** to guide them. When they get close to land, lighthouses and marker **buoys** help ships get to port safely.

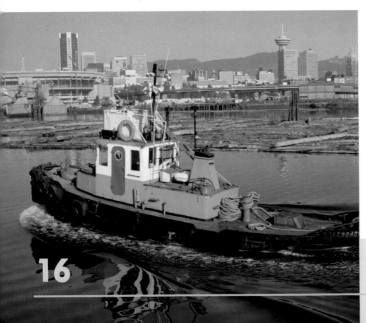

Tugboat

Tugboats guide large ships into port.

Icebreakers are special boats that can travel through ice fields.

Energy from the Sea

Some of the oil and natural gas we use comes from beneath the sea. Oil and gas are fossil fuels that people use to make heat and power.

Fossil fuels are the remains of long-dead plants and animals. Millions of years ago plants and tiny sea creatures died and sank to the bottom of the ocean. The plants and animals were slowly pressed together. Heat, pressure, and bacteria changed them into natural gas, coal, or oil.

Geologists drill holes in the ocean floor looking for oil and gas. When a large amount of oil or gas is found, a platform is built in the open sea. Narrow holes are drilled into the seabed. The oil or gas is then pumped to the surface. Oil is loaded into big ships called tankers. Natural gas is sent to the shore by pipeline.

There are large oil platforms in the ocean.

Large pipes carry gas across the land for use or for storage.

These men are drilling for oil on an oil rig.

Food from the Sea

People have always caught fish and other sea creatures using baskets, hooks, and nets. Plants and salt are also collected from the sea.

Today, large fishing boats can catch, clean, and freeze fish while still at sea. Modern fishing boats take huge amounts of seafood from the sea. Every year more than 75 million tons of fish such as tuna, cod, and snapper are caught worldwide.

Seaweed is also **harvested**. People eat it raw or cooked and sometimes use it to thicken foods such as ice cream and yogurt. Seaweed can also be used to make toothpaste!

In some hot countries, people trap seawater in shallow ponds. The sun and wind dry up the water leaving behind the salt. The salt is collected and used to season and preserve food.

Fish seller

Large fishing boats use a tracking system called sonar to find large schools of fish.

Many people use small boats to go fishing.

This man is harvesting seaweed.

21

Using the Sea

Recreation

Transportation

Energy

Food

Glossary

atmosphere	the mixture of gases that surrounds Earth
buoy	an anchored marker that floats
fossil fuel	remains of plants and animals that have turned into oil, coal, or gas
geologist	a scientist who studies the earth
harvested	gathered grains or other live foods
navigate	find the way
radar	equipment that uses radio waves to determine position
satellite	an object orbiting Earth that sends and receives information
scuba	stands for **s**elf **c**ontained **u**nderwater **b**reathing **a**pparatus
shipping lanes	regular routes that ships follow
sonar	equipment that uses sound waves to determine depth or position
tsunami	large waves caused by an undersea disturbance
water pressure	the pressing weight of water above

Index